IN
TE

2
15

This

A Day in the Life: Rainforest Animals

Orangutan

Anita Ganeri

www.raintreepublishers.co.uk
Visit our website to find out more information about Raintree books.

To order:
☎ Phone 0845 6044371
🖹 Fax +44 (0) 1865 312263
🖳 Email myorders@raintreepublishers.co.uk

Customers from outside the UK please telephone +44 1865 312262

Raintree is an imprint of Capstone Global Library Limited, a company incorporated in England and Wales having its registered office at 7 Pilgrim Street, London, EC4V 6LB – Registered company number: 6695582

Edited by Nancy Dickmann, Rebecca Rissman, and Catherine Veitch
Designed by Steve Mead
Picture research by Mica Brancic
Originated by Capstone Global Library
Printed and bound in China by South China Printing Company Ltd

ISBN 978 1 4062 1785 8 (hardback)
14 13 12 11 10
10 9 8 7 6 5 4 3 2 1

British Library Cataloguing in Publication Data
Ganeri, Anita
Orangutan. -- (A day in the life. Rainforest animals)
599.8'83-dc22
A full catalogue record for this book is available from the British Library.

Acknowledgements
We would like to thank the following for permission to reproduce photographs: Alamy **p. 10** (© Jeroen Hendriks); Ardea **pp. 11, 22** (Thomas Marent); Corbis **pp. 4, 23 mammal** (© Theo Allofs), **6** (© Tom Brakefield), **7, 23 pouch** (© DLILLC), **17** (© W. Perry Conway), **19** (© Warren Jacobi), **21** (epa/© FRISO GENTSCH); FLPA **pp. 5, 23 ape** (Jurgen & Christine Sohns), **12, 23 rubbery** (Minden Pictures/Jeffrey Oonk/FN), **13** (Minden Pictures/Cyril Ruoso), **15, 18** (Minden Pictures/Thomas Marent); Nature Picture Library **pp. 14, 20, 23 vine** (© Anup Shah); Photolibrary **pp. 9** (David Maitland), **16** (imagebroker.net/ROM ROM); Shutterstock **p. 23 rainforest** (© Szefei).

Cover photograph of an adult orangutan with an infant reproduced with permission of Corbis (© Frans Lanting).

Back cover photographs of (left) a male orangutan reproduced with permission of Corbis (© DLILLC); and (right) an orangutan's nest reproduced with permission of Nature Picture Library (© Anup Shah).

We would like to thank Michael Bright for his invaluable help in the preparation of this book.

Contents

Some words are in bold, **like this**. You can find them in the glossary on page 23.

An orangutan is a **mammal**.

Many mammals have hairy bodies and feed their babies milk.

chimpanzee

Orangutans belong to a group of mammals called **apes**.

Chimpanzees and gorillas are also types of apes.

What are orangutans look like?

Orangutans have large bodies that are covered in long, red-brown hair.

They have very long, strong arms.

cheek

pouch

Male orangutans are bigger than females.

An adult male has big cheeks and a baggy **pouch** around its neck.

Where do orangutans live?

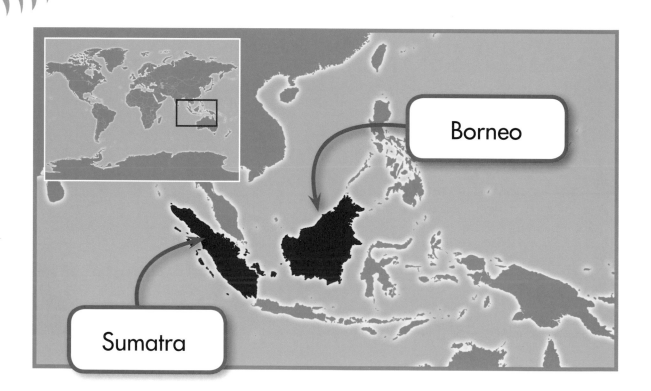

Borneo

Sumatra

Orangutans live on the islands of Borneo and Sumatra in South East Asia.

They live in the **rainforests** that grow on the islands.

Orangutans spend most of their time high up in the rainforest trees.

They do not come down to the ground very often.

An orangutan wakes up when the Sun rises.

It has a snack of fruit for breakfast.

After breakfast, the orangutan has a short rest before it starts the day.

Then it spends most of the day looking for food among the trees.

What do orangutans eat and drink?

Orangutans mainly eat fruit, leaves, and other parts of plants.

An orangutan picks a fruit, then peels it with its teeth and **rubbery** lips.

It rains every day in the **rainforest**.

When an orangutan feels thirsty, it scoops up rainwater from a hole in a tree to drink.

How do orangutans move about?

vine

An orangutan rocks on a branch or **vine**.

It does this until it is close enough to grab another branch or vine.

hand

The orangutan always holds on to a tree with at least one hand and one foot.

Its hands and feet are shaped like hooks for grabbing hold of the branches.

Why do orangutans live alone?

Male orangutans usually live on their own.

They do not help to look after young orangutans.

A young orangutan lives with its mother until it is about eight years old.

Its mother teaches it where to find food in the **rainforest**.

A male orangutan can be very noisy.

He can puff up his neck **pouch** and make a loud roaring sound.

This sound can be heard far away in the **rainforest**.

It warns other orangutans to stay away from the tree where the male is feeding.

W---t ---r--.. --t--.. at night?

nest

In the evening, an orangutan builds a nest in the trees with leaves and twigs.

The nest is where the orangutan sleeps.

Baby orangutans are born in the nest at night.

When they are older, their mother shows them how to make nests.

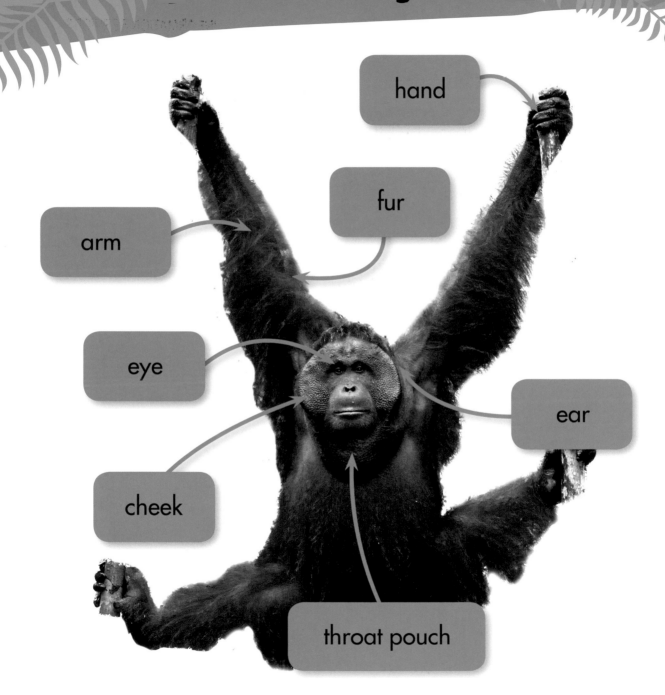

hand

fur

arm

eye

ear

cheek

throat pouch

Glossary

 **ape** large, human-like mammal, such as an orangutan or a chimpanzee

 **mammal** animal that feeds its babies milk. Most mammals have hair or fur.

 **pouch** baggy piece of skin

 **rainforest** thick forest with very tall trees and a lot of rain

 **rubbery** soft and bendy

 **vine** long, dangling plant that grows in the rainforest

Fi... ...t m...r

Books

Rainforest Animals (Focus on Habitats), Stephen Savage
  (Wayland, 2006)
Orangutans (Animals in Danger)
  (Ticktock Media Ltd, 2006)

Websites

www.orangutans-sos.org/kids/orangutan_facts/
http://kids.nationalgeographic.com/Animals/CreatureFeature/
  Orangutan

Index